A BRIEF OUTLINE OF THE GRAMMAR OF THE TUDA LANGUAGE

A BRIEF OUTLINE
OF THE
GRAMMAR
OF THE
TUDA LANGUAGE

G. U. POPE

GYAN

Published by

Gyan Publishing House
5, Ansari Road
Daryaganj, New Delhi-110002
Phone: 011-47034999, 9811692060
E-mail: books@gyanbooks.com

Distribution Network
gyanbooks.com
India, USA, Canada, UK, Australia, France

ISBN : 978-81-212-4253-0 (PB)

2nd Impression 2020

Printed at: Gyan Press, Delhi.

A Brief Outline of the Grammar of the Tuda Language
Author: G. U. Pope

A BRIEF OUTLINE

OF THE

GRAMMAR

OF THE

TUDA LANGUAGE

BY THE

REV. G. U. POPE, D.D.,

FELLOW OF THE MADRAS UNIVERSITY, MEMBER OF THE GERMAN ORIENTAL SOCIETY.

[*From a collection of Tuda words and sentences presented by the Rev. Friedrich Metz, of the Basel Missionary Society.*]

NOTICE.

These outlines are the result of a good deal of personal intercourse with the Tuḍas, during a residence of twelve years on the Nílagiris. With the kind assistance of the late lamented J. W. Breeks, Esq., the First Commissioner of the Nílagiris, the subject of the Tuḍa language was investigated a few years ago in connection with a small Archæological Society in Ootacamund. At the request of Colonel Marshall, I have put the results into this shape, to be printed in his work on the Tuḍas. I think that the facts of the language are here gathered together. It is becoming daily more difficult to ascertain what is originally Tuda and what is borrowed by that people from the later immigrants.

In one or two matters, I have ventured to differ from the Rev. Dr. Caldwell, whose Drâviḍian Grammar has invested such researches with a new interest. I advance my opinions with unfeigned diffidence. While agreeing in the main with that profound scholar, I yet think that the remarkable analogies between the Keltic and the Drâviḍian languages merit a more thorough investigation.

CHAPTER XXIX.

OUTLINES

OF THE

TUDA GRAMMAR.

I. THE ALPHABET.

§ 1. THE TUḌA LANGUAGE has no compositions, written or unwritten, not a ballad nor a scrap of anything to indicate intellectual activity. The Tuḍas, like their buffalos, are fine animals; but they are the least cultivated of the Drâvidian races. CHAP. XXIX.

No trace remains of the employment by them of any written character: it is probable, therefore, that they separated from the other Drâviḍians before the 'ur-sprache' of those tribes was reduced to writing.

§ 2. This language, of which but a very scanty fragment remains in use, has more sounds than any other Drâviḍian dialect, and some of these are peculiar to it, seeming to have been modified by the position and habits of the tribe.

The Tuḍas chiefly converse in the open air, calling to each other from one breezy hill-top to another. Their speech sounds like Old Kanarese spoken in the teeth of a gale of wind.

CHAP. XXIX.

§ 3. The vowels are:

SHORT.	LONG.
1. **a**, as in 'America.' Ex. **atham**, *he*.	6. **â**, as **aw**, in 'bawl.' Ex. **âḷ**, *a man*.
2. **i**, as in 'pin.' Ex. **nim**, *your*.	7. **î**, as in 'pique.' Ex. **nî**, *thou*.
3. **u**, as in 'Cooḳ.' Ex. **ulg**, *within*.	8. **û**, as in 'School.' Ex. **mûdu**, *three*.
4. **e**, as in 'hem.' Ex. **yenak**, *to me*.	9. **ê**, as **a** in 'pale.' Ex. **êt**, *why?*
5. **o**, as in 'opinion.' Ex. **kor**, *cold*.	10. **ô**, as in 'opium.' Ex. **ôm**, *we*.

Some of these are occasionally modified; thus,

ö sounds as in German, or as **eu** in French, in 'fleur.'

Ex. **tökh**, *female*.

ü, as in German, or as **u** in French, in 'pur.'

Ex. **ütsh**, *five*.

u, at the end of a word, has a very fine sound, approaching to an **i**. The Drâviḍian 'half **u**.'

a, in the last syllable of a word, sounds like a very short **e**.

ô and **â** are almost always interchangeable: thus, the Kanarese *kâl* is in Tuḍa **kôl**.

§ 4. The Consonants are:

1. **k**, as in 'kalendar.' Ex. **âḍken**, *I play*.
2. **g**, as in 'gun.' Ex. **avaḷg**, *to her*.
3. **k'h**, as in 'blockhead.' Ex. **mokh**, *a son*.
4. **g'h**, as in 'loghouse.' Ex. any final **g** may be aspirated.
5. **j**, as in 'jam.' Ex. **majjal**, *yellow*.
6. **ch**, as in 'chin.' Ex. **chen**, *red*.
7. **t**, as in 'ten.' Ex. **terigi**, *again*.
8. **th**, as in 'this.' Ex. **atham**, *he*.
9. **th**, as in 'thin.' Ex. **nilthken**, *I stand*.
10. **d**, as in 'dog.' Ex. **nâd**, *wet*.
11. **ṭ**, lingual. Ex. **muṭṭiken**, *I feel*.
12. **ḍ**, lingual. Ex. **kûḍa**, *together*.
13. **p**, as in 'pen.' Ex. **pui**, *strike*.

14. **f**, as in 'fun.' Ex. **pûf**, *an insect.*
15. **b**, as in 'bull.' Ex. **boath**, *a conical temple.*
16. **v**, as in 'very.' Ex. **vêr**, *another.*
17. **b'h**. Ex. **bhût**, *a demon.*
18. **m**, as in 'man.' Ex. **âm**, *Tuesday.*
19. **n**, as in 'no.' Ex. **tani**, *Saturday.*
20. **l**, hard, lingual. Ex. **beḷḷi**, *Friday.*
21. **r**, hard, lingual. Ex. **âṛ**, *six.*
22. **s**. Ex. **âsvom**, *Sunday.*
23. **sh**. Ex. **ütsh**, *five.*
24. **zh**. Ex. **êlzh**, *seven.*

§ 5. It is difficult to decide whether all these sounds belong to the Tuḍa itself. The aspirates especially, except **kh** and **ch**, are, it may be suspected, foreign to it.

§ 6. Some of them seem to have arisen from the lingual **ṛ**, which is found in all the South-Indian languages, and which existed in the oldest forms of the Drâviḍian. In Madras it is sounded **y**, and in Tinnevelly **l**. In Telugu it is softened into **r**, or changed into **t** or **d**. It is a kind of triple **r**, sounded very far back in the throat, thus seeming to be a mixture of **r**, **l**, and **z**.

It resembles the Welsh **ll**. (Comp. § 43.)

Thus Kan. *êḷu*	and Tam. êṛu, *seven*,	make	in Tuḍa	**elzh**.
„ *kiḷ*	„ kiṛ, *under*	„	„	**kirzh**.
„ *buruḍe*	„ puṛuti, *mud*	„	„	**purzh**.

§ 7. It may be stated as a rule that the Tuḍa **sh** and **zh**, (which are strong linguals) generally represent a final **l** or **ḷ** of the Kanarese:

Old Kan. and Tam.	*pal* (*lu*)	in Tuḍa	**parsh**.
„	„ *âḷi*, *âri*, circle	„	**ârsh**.
„	„ *bil* (*lu*), *vil*, a bow	„	**virzh**.
„	„ *puli*, tiger	„	**pürsh**.

§ 8. Sometimes **sh** is the equivalent for the other linguals; thus,

Old Kan. and Tam. *karaḍi*, a bear, is **karṣh**.

CHAP. XXIX.

§ 9. The letter **f** is pronounced by the Tuḍas full and clear, while any other Drâviḍian race would pronounce 'first' as *pirsht*, the sound of sharp **f** being unknown to them; as are some other sharp sounds, such as *th* in *thin*, and *s* in *sin*.

I think the Tuḍa f sound has arisen, as in English, from the corruption of a guttural or lingual.

Enough has become with us *enuf*.

So the Tuḍa **pûf**, 'an insect,' is probably Old Kan. *purlu*.

It must, however, be stated that the words in which **f** is found are precisely those which it is most difficult to trace. Thus,

mituf is 'nose' (? Kan. *mitte*, 'projecting').
mâf is a 'Baḍagan' (? (Kan.) *mâva*, 'father-in-law,' (used as a term of respect).
or a 'deer' (? *mân*).

§ 10. The lingual ḍ of the Kan. is in Tuḍa sometimes represented by r; thus,

nar-k-en, 'I walk.' (Kan. root *naḍ*).
nôr, 'district.' (Kan. nâḍ).

§ 11. **Th** (as in *thin*) and **sh** (lingual) are often euphonically (?) inserted in Tuda words. This is quite a Tuda peculiarity.

The former sound is not at all Drâviḍian (though it is Keltic); and the latter is only found in the other D. dialects in Sanskrit derivatives.

Sh is, however, quite the favourite Tuda sound.

Thus, **nilthken**, *I stand*. (§ 26.)
K. **Nil** + temp. part. **k** + inflectionable part. **en**

Here **th** is a mere euphonic insertion.

Ershken, *I am*.
R. **er** + K. + **en**.

Here, too, **sh** is probably a mere euphonic insertion.

§ 12. In Tuḍa **v** or **w** is optionally pronounced before **o** initial; thus, **vodd**=*one*; but in the compound we find **oddi-adi**= *alone* (lit. one-step); and **on** or **or** is the Drâviḍian root. So in English 'one' is pronounced 'won.'

The possession of this sound of **w** is one of the many noteworthy analogies between the Keltic languages and the Drâviḍian.

So **y** may, as in the other Drâv. dialects, be prefixed to any word beginning with **e**. Thus, **enak** or **yenak**=*to me.*

This, too, is found in English, and is probably due to Keltic influences: *ewe* is pronounced *yew.*

NOUNS.

§ 13. Tuḍa nouns have no inflections for number or gender.

§ 14. The Nominative, Accusative, Vocative, and Genitive cases are alike, being the unaltered root.

§ 15. The inflectional particles in use are, (1) for the dative, **g** or **k**: (2) for the instrumental ablative and the ablative of remotion, **end** (or **edd**); and (3) for the local ablative **orzh**.

These correspond very exactly to the Old Kanarese, *ge*, *inda*, and *oḷ* (comp. § 43).

§ 16. The following is a **Paradigm** of a Tuḍa noun:

	âḷ, *a man*
N. Acc. Voc. Gen.	**âḷ**, *a man*
Dat.	**âḷg**, *to* or *for a man*
Abl. (instrum. and remotion)	**âḷend** (**âḷedd**), *by* or *from a man*
(place) . . .	**âḷorzh**, *in a man.*

§ 17. Since the nominative, accusative, and genitive cases are alike, it is chiefly by position that the syntax of a Tuḍa sentence is regulated. A noun immediately before a transitive verb is the object; while a noun before another noun is in the genitive case, or qualifies it like an adjective.

CHAP. XXIX.

In the latter case **ad**, the root of the epicene pronoun of the 3rd person, appears to be sometimes inserted, making what looks like a genitive case.

This resembles the Kan. usage. In that language, certain nouns add **d** to the root to form the inflectional base, which is used for any case. The Tamil adds *thu* (*th* flat) to the root to form a genitive.

§ 18. The Tuḍa pronouns are irregular, but correspond very closely to those of the other Drâviḍian dialects.

§ 19. THE PERSONAL PRONOUNS.

(1) The pronoun of the 1st person.

	SINGULAR.	PLURAL.
Nom.	**ân**, *I*	**ôm, âm**, *we*
Acc.	**yen**, *me*	**yem, âm**, *us*
Gen.	**yen** ; **yen-adu**, *my*, *mine*	**yem** ; **yem-adu**, *our*, *ours*
Dat.	**yen-ak**, *to* or *for me*	**yem-ak**, *to* or *for us*
Abl.	**yen-end**, **-edd** } *from me.*	**yem-end**, **âm-end**, **âm-edd** } *from us*

NOTE.—The original form of the Drâviḍian pronoun of the 1st person is uncertain.

(1.) In the oldest dialect of Tamil and in Tulu it is *yán*, in Old Kanarese án, in Old Telugu ênu, in Malayalim nján.

(2.) The inflections of this pronoun in nearly all the cognate languages have *en*; and in the oldest forms *y* is prefixed at pleasure to all cases beginning with *e*.

(3.) The pronoun when appended to the Drâviḍian verb in *an*, *en*, ini, eni, én.

(4.) In later Tamil Kanarese and Telugu we find forms nân, nâm, and nénu, in the Nom. Singular; and nâm, mému in the Nom. Plural. This *n* or *m* I do not regard as primitive, since it is wanting in all the old forms. The Drâviḍian languages prefix *n* to several words which they have received from other languages. Thus the Sanskrit *yuga* is in Tamil *nugam*; and *nangûram* is the form in which the word *anchor* has settled down in the Drâviḍian dialects. I can see how *n* might have crept in; I cannot imagine its disappearance from every ancient dialect.

(5.) This is not the place for a full discussion of the subject; but I would compare *ân* with the very ancient form S. *aham*.

Nor can I think it clear that ôm is not related to the Sanskrit *vayam*, or to the Greek ἡμεῖς or ἄμμες, and Védic *asmé*.

§ 20. (2) The pronoun of the 2nd person.

CHAP. XXIX.

	SINGULAR.	PLURAL.
Nom. Voc.	**nî**	**nim-a**
Acc. Gen.	**nin**	**nim**
Dat.	**nin-ak**	**nim-ak** / **nim, nim-adu**
Abl.	**nin-end** or **nin-edd**, *by* or *from thee* / **nin-orzh**, *in thee*	**nim-end, nim-edd** / **nim-oṛzh**

This closely resembles the ancient Kanarese and Tamil.

I do not know whether it is of use to point out the Drâviḍian root *nil*, 'stand,' with its past part. in Kan. *ninu*, as the possible origin of this pronoun.

Here **n** is, I think, undoubtedly radical.

§ 21. The pronoun of the 3rd person in Tuḍa (which is really a demonstrative pronoun, or adjective) has the peculiarity, that like the Latin *se*, it has no inflection for gender or number.

Thus **atham**=*he, she, it, they*.

[Generally *m* is an indistinct nasal, the anuswâra of the Sanskrit.]

It is declined like âl (§ 16).

N. A. G.	**atham**
Dat.	**athan-g**
Abl.	**ath-end, atham-edd, athamend** / **atham-orzh, ath-orzh.**

The resemblance to S. **adas** is remarkable.

Kan. **âtanu**=he ; **adu**=it.

It will be remarked that the verbal forms of the 3rd person make no distinction of number or gender. (Comp. § 26.)

This is a remote demonstrative (ille, &c.) ; **itham** is used for the proximate (hic, &c.).

CHAP. XXIX.

Besides this oldest form the Tuda uses the pronouns

avan (ille); **ivan** (hic)
aval (illa); **ival** (hæc)
with their plurals
avar; **ivar**, which are declined like **âl**, with the addition of a kind of genitive in *du*: avandu, &c.

Here **avan**, &c., are the remote demonstratives, and **ivan**, &c., the proximate demonstratives.

These appear to be forms recently introduced, or, it may be, reintroduced into Tuda from Kanarese or Tamil.

Avandu=avan+du, and is prefixed to a noun adjectivally, and so forms a kind of genitive case: *avandu kukh*=his wife. (§ 17.)

The use of **a** and **i** as demonstrative prefixes is thoroughly Drâviḍian.

The root of this pronoun is evidently **d**.

§ 22. TUḌA ADVERBS.

(1) Words answering to English adverbs exist in Tuḍa. Some of them are also used as nouns, some are parts of the verb.

(2) The following list includes nearly all that are in use.

1. *yes*	**hâ**	These seem to be really interjections.
2. *no*	**âha**	
3. *here, there, where*	**ite, ate, ete**	Here the *i*, *a*, *e*, as demonstrative and interrogative particles appear.
4. *why*	**ête**	T. and K.
5. *how*	**yetete**	Reduplicate of ete. (3.)
6. *who, what?*	**athario**	Atham=*it*, âr=*who*? ô an interrogative particle.
7. *above*	**mêl, mok**	*Mêl* is Drâviḍian. **Mok** from Sansk.=*before*.
8. *below*	**kîl, erk**	Kan. keḷa, irrida. Tam. kîr, irrakka.
9. *before* (place)	**mud**	Drâvid. *mun*, mundu.
before (time)	**much**	Kan. *munche*.

10. *behind*	**pinne**	A. Kan. *pinde.*
11. *outside*	**porram**	A. Kan. pora. purram in T.
12. *inside*	**ulg**	Uḷ, *within*, in the dative case.
13. *much* 14. *more* [comp. (23)=*yet much*]	**upâm** **innupâm**	A. K. *ubbarige.* In Kan. Tam. and Tel. *up* or *ub* is a root signifying increase. Comp. Sansk. upari.
15. *near*	**kekhuri**	This seems to be a corruption of Kan. *kaige* oḷ=*in hand* or *at hand.*
16. *far*	**bathki**	*Badike*=near, in K.
17. *also, together*	**kûḍa**	Infin. of Kûḍu, *come together.*
18. *alone*	**oddi-aḍi**	Odd=one. aḍi=*step,' a time.*
19. *frequently*	**upâm-aḍi**	Comp. (13)=more-step.
20. *soon, suddenly*	**birnd**	Kan. biri-biri (§ 34.)
21. *again*	**terigi**	Kan. *tirige.*
22. *enough*	**ettana**	In Tamil=*this much.* Kan. ittani=the whole
23. *yet*	**in**	Kan. *innu*, more, yet.
24. *when* 25. *then* 26. *now*	**etwan** **atwan** **itwan**	Compare (3).
27. *for ever*	**etwan-etwan**	Lit.=when- when.
28. *another*	**in odd**=yet one.	

§ 23. TUḌA ADJECTIVES.

(1) There are a few words which appear to **be adjectives** by **nature ; but the** majority **are** merely **nouns placed before other nouns to qualify or limit their meaning.**

(2) The following list contains some of the **adjectives now in common use.**

1. *good* 2. *pretty*	**uḷthe** **nal**	*oḷ, oḷḷi, oḷḷida*, in Kan. ***thi*=*thu*** or ***du*** or ***di***, *nal* in O. Kan., and Tam., and in the other Drâv. dialects.
3. *old*	**keḷ**	*Kiṛa* in Tam., ***kerr*** in O. Kan.

CHAP. XXIX.

4. *big*	**êt-ud**	*ètt*=elevation, in Tamil. In Kan. *ḕḷda*=having risen	*ud* in *ètud* and in *kirud* is evidently *athạm* =it.
5. *little*	**kin, kir-ud**	Tam. *çin, çirridu.* Kan. *kin, kir*	
6. *hot*	**bîrsh**	Kan. *bisi, bishi, bisilu*	
7. *cold*	**kor**	Drâviḍian root is *kuḷ*	
8. *wet*	**nâd**	This is Kan. *nâd, nân, nând*	
9. *dry*	**voṇag**	K. *oṇa, oṇagu.* In Tam. *uṇa*	This *g* or *gu* a strengthening part. in K. and T.
10. *male*	**têk-an**	*an* is the Drâv. masc. term.	Here seems to be an internal modification of a root to distinguish gender.
11. *female*	**tökh**	These words cannot be traced to any Drâviḍian root. *dêham*=body. *tô-gai* is a poet. word for woman	
12. *white*	**bel-thi** / **belp**	Kan. *beḷ*	
13. *red*	**chen** / **bäkh-gudi** / **kandati** / **kepu**	Kan. *chen*, kudi, *kanda. kempu*	
14. *yellow*	**majjal**	Tam. *manjal*	
15. *black, blue, green*	**kar-thti**	Kan. *kari*	
16. *other*	**vêr**	Kan. *bère.* Tam. *vêrru.*	
17. *great*	**perud**		

(3) These roots, probably among the oldest in the language, are, with hardly an exception, common to all the Drâviḍian languages; but the peculiarities of the Kanarese are found in the Tuḍa.

§ 24. Forms answering to the comparative and superlative degrees are obtained by putting a noun in the 'ablative of remotion' before the adjective; and by prefixing the adverb **upâm**=much. CHAP. XXIX.

Thus: **athumed-kirud**, *smaller than it*
âḷed-êtud, *greater than a man*
upâm-êtud, upâmkiruḍ, *greatest, smallest*

§ 25. THE TUḌA VERBS.

(1) The Tuḍa verb has I. an affirmative form consisting of an indicative mood and an imperative mood; II. a negative form, with the same two moods.

(2) It has two tenses: I. An indefinite tense, which is present or future; II. A past tense.

(3) There are fragments of other forms which can only be conjecturally restored.

§ 26. The verb '*to be*' is thus inflected.

Root **er**.

I. Affirmative Form.

Indicative Mood.

(I) Indefinite Present.

Singular.	Plural.
1. **(ân) er–sh–k–en**, *I am*	**(ôm) er–sh–k–imi**
2. **(nî) er–sh–ch–i**	**(nima) er–sh–ch–i**
3. **(avan) er–sh–ch–i**	**(avar) er–sh–ch–i.**

(II) Indefinite Past.

Singular.	Plural.
1 **(ân) edd–er–sh–p–ini**, *I was*	**(ôm) edd–er–sh–p–imi**
2 **(nî)** } **edd–er–sh–ch–i**	**(nima)** } **edd–er–sh–ch–i**
3 **(avan).** }	**(avar)** }

This is evidently a compound form obtained by prefixing **edd** to the present tense: **edd** being for **erd.** (§ 30.)

The 1st pers. sing. takes what seems to be an alternative form in **p-ini**: **ershpini=ershken.**

Sh is the Tuḍa substitute for **k** : **shk**=**kk**
Ch is a softened form of **k** : so in Saxon, **spec**=*speech*
sceal=*shall.*

Imperative Mood.

iru, *be thou*
ir-mâ, *let it be.*

Of this **mâ** I can give no explanation.

II. Negative Form.

(I) Indefinite Present : *I, &c., am not.*

	Singular.	Plural.
1.	ir-eni	ir-emi
2.	ir-e	ir-e
3.	ir-adi	ir-adi

(II) Indefinite Past : *I, &c., was not.*

1.	er-th-eni	er-th-emi
2.	er-th-e	er-th-e
3.	er-th-adi	er-th-adi

§ 27. The Verb **âḍ**, *dance*, is thus inflected.

I. Affirmative Form.

Indicative Mood.

(I) Indefinite Present : *I, &c., dance.*

	Singular.	Plural.
1.	âḍ-k-en	âḍ-k-emi
2.	âḍ-ch-i	âḍ-ch-i
3.	âḍ-ch-i	âḍ-ch-i

(II) Indefinite Past : *I, &c., dancea.*

1.	âḍ-th-b-ini	âḍ-th-b-imi
2. 3.	âḍ-th-ch-i	âḍ-th-ch-i

Imperative Mood.

pui, *strike* !
pui mâ, *let him strike* !

II. Negative Form.

Indicative Mood.

(I) Indefinite Present : *I, &c., dance not.*

	Singular.	Plural.
1.	âḍ-eni	âḍ-emi
2.	âḍ-e	âḍ-e
3.	áḍ-adi	áḍ-adi

(II) Indefinite Past : *I, &c., danced not.*

1.	âṭa ger-th-eni	âṭa ger-th-emi
2.	âṭa ger-th-e	âṭa ger-th-e
3.	âṭa ger-th-adi	âṭa ger-th-adi

Imperative Mood.

pui ad iru } *strike not!*
pui âṭu }

N.B. Of these, one is Kan. and the other Tamil.

§ 28. It will be seen from these paradigms that the Tuḍa like the other Drâviḍian dialects, has *temporal particles,* which are inserted between the root and the personal terminations. In the present tense affirmative the temporal particle is K, which is softened into CH (as in *Chúrch*), before I.

In the 1st persons S. and P. a *p* or *b* (it is pronounced both ways) is occasionally found. This may have some connexion with the temporal particle found in the present, in Old Kanarese, which is DAP.

This is almost the only part of the Tuḍa language that seems to indicate great antiquity. It is, however, Old Kanarese.

In ordinary Kanarese there is scarcely a trace of the *k,* which being softened into *h,* or *v,* has finally disappeared.

In Tamil it remains in the temporal particle of the present *Kirru* or *Girru*; in a strengthening particle *gu* added to many roots; and in some old poetical forms, such as *çey-gu*= I will do ; *çey-gum,* we will do.

CHAP. XXIX. In Malayalim it is still found in the present of many verbs: in the form of *kunnu.*

In the old form Kanarese *bé-ku,* 'must,' it is preserved; as also in *çâ-ku,* 'it is enough.'

In Old Kanarese *kum* and *gum* may be appended to any root to form an aorist This admits no variation for number or person. Thus *avar mâḍugum*=they do.

In the past the *temporal particle* is TH (as in *thin*). This is *d* in Kanarese.

The negative mode is obtained by joining the root to the personal termination without the intervention of any temporal particle. This is common to all the Drâviḍian languages.

§ 29. The personal terminations are for the

	SINGULAR.	PLURAL.
I. Pers.	*en, eni, ini*	*imi, emi*
II. Pers.	*i, e*	
III. Pers.	*i, adi*	

These are shortened forms of the pronouns. See §§ 19–21.

§ 30. There are also in Tuḍa traces of other verbal forms which are peculiar to the Drâviḍian family of languages.

The relative participle, or adjective form of the verb, is one of these.

In the day when I joined, is in Tuḍa:

ân kûḍid nâḷorzh
[*I joined day-in*].

Here *kûḍid* is in Kanarese *kûḍida,* and is called a 'relative participle,' qualifying *day,* and being equivalent to *when (I) joined,* thus including in itself the relative adverb.

So, **ân âḍid nâḷ**, *the day I danced.*
Thus **edd** is=Kan. *idda,* 'which was.' (§ 26.)

§ 31. Tuḍa also forms a verbal noun, a kind of infinitive, from verbs ending in a flat consonant by changing the flat into its corresponding sharp, as in all the other Drâviḍian languages. CHAP XXIX.

Thus âḍ, *dance* or *play*, makes

âṭa, *dancing* [Tam. aḍu, aṭṭam; Kan. áḍu, áṭa, and in Tel. the same].

The past tense of the negative form is thus:

âṭa ger-ṭh-eni
dancing did-(not)-I. (§ 27.)

And here (1) Is not *ger-th* singularly like the Sanskrit *krita*, done! Surely this is the KAR of the Indo-Germanic 'grund-sprache.'.
(2) May this not throw light on the Tamil temporal particle *kirra*? and probably on the K. (§ 28.)
(3) Does it not seem that the negative particle in such forms is really dropped? The emphatic 'dancing-did-I' remains, and the formula of negation has perished. (Comp. Earle's Philology of the English Tongue, p. 427.)

§ 32. In examining the forms of the verb still surviving among the Tuḍas, it becomes evident that many verbal inflections have been dropped. We have, it seems, but the débris of an elaborate inflectional system. There was probably a future tense with *temporal particle* **v, p,** or **b,** as in Kanarese and Tamil. This has disappeared, as in Saxon, and the present (like the English indefinite present) is now used as a future with an adverb. The forms **âḍ-th-b-ini** and **er-sh-p-imi** are probably remnants of it (§ 27.)

§ 33. An infinitive mood in **a** perhaps existed; for the adverb **kûḍa** is the infinitive of **kûḍ,** unless indeed this is a word of recent importation. (§ 22.)

§ 34. The adverb *birnd*, 'suddenly,' seems to be from a root which is found in Old Kanarese. *biri*, 'burst,' and in

CHAP. XXIX. Tamil *viṛu*, 'fall,' from which, in the latter dialect, the past adv. participle, *viṛundu*, is formed. There is, therefore, a trace of a *past adv.* part. (§ 22.)

§ 35. There is no passive inflection in Tuḍa.

§ 36. The interrogative forms are obtained by adding **â**, which, as in Tamil and in Old Kanarese, is the chief interrogative particle.

Thus *has Beḷiâni joined?* is, **Beḷiâni kûḍthiyâ**?

ê and **ô** are also interrogative letters in Tuḍa.

§ 37. It is not easy to decide whether the Tuḍa retains any trace of a subjunctive mood.

The following sentence seems to contain something equivalent to it.

Atham Nastufig kûḍâ vaḷi, kukh in odd âḷk ûdthchi
He to Nastufi not joining (marrying) when, (the) woman yet one man has married.
If he do not marry Nastufi, she will marry another man.

Here **kûḍâ** is apparently a negative participle qualifying the noun **vaḷı**=time (Kan. *vêḷe*).

The forms **pôk-âdi** and **pôk-ârzh** are found with the meaning *of go.* Here **âdi** and **ârzh** are joined to the root. They seem to be the Kan. **arê** or Tam. **âl**. But they are probably borrowed from Tamil.

The verbal root is the imperative of 2nd pers. sing.; thus, âḍ, *play thou.* Another form adds mâ to the root; thus, pui-mâ, *strike thou.*

§ 38. The Tuḍa has neither prepositions nor conjunctions. This want of 'link words' is an index of the entire absence of the habit of reasoning.

§ 39. By way of illustration. I added a few sentences.

SENTENCES.

(The words are in the subjoined lists.)

(1) When I married Beḷiâni I was a widow
ân Beḷiânig kúḍid nâḷorzh ân barudi.
I to-Beḷiâni joined in-day I widow.

(2) Is Nastufi married?
Nastufig beḷthta gavthyâ?
to-Nastufi silver tied?
beḷthta=*silver badge.* (In Kan. beḷḷe=*silver*+(?) tâli=*marriage token.*)

gavthyâ=*gavth*+â or yâ.
This seems to be an adv. part.=*having tied* (§ 34) followed by the interrog. (§ 36).

(3) Is Beḷiâni married?
Beḷiâni kukhag kûdṭhyâ?
Beḷiâni to-a woman joined?
kukhag. Here *a* is inserted to connect **kukh** with its case ending *g*.

(4) Your wife walks not with my wife.
Nin kaṭṭ-vodi-kukh yen kaṭṭ-vodi—kukh naḍevadi.
nade vadi (§ 27). Kan. nade=*walk.*
v is a Euphonic insertion.

(5) My uncle's sons are my brothers.
Yen perudên kirudên mokh yeṇ aṇan taman
My great-father little-father son my elder-brother younger-brother
erhschi.
are.

yen (§ 19) **perud, kirud** (§ 23).
aṇan (K. aṇa=*elder brother.* The R. seem to mean *above.*)
taman (K. tamma=*younger brother*).
ên (K. ayya=*father, priest*).
ershchi (§ 26).

The final **n**, as the termination of masculine nouns, here seems to be fairly in the language; but I suspect it is only an obscure nasal, not differing from the epicene ending **m** in **atham.**

CHAP XXIX.

(6) That one's father and this one's father are brothers-in-law (relatives)

atham ên itham ên bêâḷ

That father this father related-man

atham, itham (§ 21)

bêâl (bê the root of the Kan. Impersonal verb *béku*+âḷ (§ 16)).

It will be seen that the Tuḍas now use no conjunctions, a sign of their degeneracy. 'Link words' of all kinds are wanting. In fact, Tuda has scarcely any 'symbolic' words, except pronouns, and the smallest possible supply of these.

(7) Beḷiâni is married, but has no son.

Beḷiâni kukh kùḍthchi, mokh illaḍe edd

illade (Kan. *illada*=what is not)

edd=*having been* (§ 30)

The finite verb **ershchi** is understood.

§ 40. LISTS OF WORDS.

I. Verbal Roots.

1. *am, sit*	**er**	Dr. *ir, urr, uḷ* (Sansk. ṚI).
2. *see*	{ **kâṇ-th**	K. *kâṇ.*
	{ **nôḍ-th**	K. *nôd.*
3. *hear*	**kêḷ-th**	K. *kêḷ.*
4. *feel, touch*	**muṭṭi**	K. *muṭṭ.*
5. *taste*	**bâi kâṇ-th**	=see (with the) mouth.
6. *smell*	**mittuf kâṇ-th**	=see (with the) nose.
7. *dream*	**kanas kâṇ-th**	=I see a vision K. *kanas.*
8. *laugh*	**kar-th**	K. *chiri-chu.*
9. *weep*	**âḍ**	K. *aḷu.* T. *aṛu.* (S. *açru.*)
10. *sing*	**ka-th âḍ**	=I play a story. K. *kaṭhe.* S. *kathâ.*
11. *shout*	**A! U! bishar-th**	=I cry A! U! K. *bicchâd.*
12. *talk*	**arvorkh**	K. *alavâke*=loquacity.
13. *dance, play*	**âḍ**	K. *âḍ.*
14. *stand*	**nil-th**	K. *nil.*
15. *walk*	**naṛ**	K. *naḍ.*
16. *run*	**voḍi**	K. *ôḍ.*
17. *lie down*	**vori**	probably a variation of 25.

18. *give*	**tash**	K. *tar-u.*
19. *clean*	**ârẑp**	K. *âḷdu*=to dip ; *alasu*, to rinse.
20. *bow, salute*	**kombuddi**	K. *kumbu*+iḍu.
21. *ask*	**bind er-th**	K. *bêḍ.* Tam. *vênḍ.*
22. *strike*	**pui**	K. *poḍe.* Old Kan. *poy-u.*
23. *kill*	**kêḍigidviti**	K. *kêḍ*=destruction. O.K. *geidu*, made. Is **vi** a causal inflection ?
24. *die*	**kêdiverti**	(? Sansk. VRIT. Dr. paḍu.)
25. *sleep*	**vorikh**	K. *orag-u.*
26. *do, make*	**gei**	O. K. *gê, gei.*
27. *take*	**va-th, ba-th**	K. *hatt* or *patt.*
28. *join*	**kûḍ-th**	K. *kûḍ.*
29. *tie on*	**gav-th**	K. *kaṭṭ* (but ? *kavi*=put on).
30. *negative verb*	**il**	K. *il.*
31. *it thunders*	**yêr-th-ti**	K. *yere.*
32. *go*	**pôk,**	K.

§ 41. II. NOUNS

1. *a span*	**gèn**	(Kan. *gênu.* Tam. *jâṇ*)
2. *a foot*	**eddgên, aḍi**	(K. *aḍi*).
3. *a cubit*	**mlâ, mlâgei**	(K. *moḷa*).
4. *a pace*	**kandaf**	(?)
5. *a name*	**pêru, hesru**	(Kan.)
6. *a nickname*	**porra-hesru**	(=outside name) (Kan.)
a collection	**kûṭu**	(Kan.)
8. *medicine*	**maddu**	(K. *maddu.* Tam. *marunthu*).
9. *dowry*	**kêikuli**	
10. *friend*	**yenkâḷ**	(Lit.=a man to me, §§ 16, 19).
11. *old man*	**keḷâḷ**	(A. K. *keṛiva*, § 6).
12. *old woman*	**keḷachi**	(K. *keṛ.* Fem. term. *ti* or *chi* is Dr.).
13. *family*	**kûṭasâram**	(Sansk.)

CHAP XXIX.

14. *relation*	**anatama**	(K. *ana*=elder brother; *tama*=younger brother).
	pâltiâḷ	(K. *pâl*).
	pâyâl	(K. *bê*+*âl*).
15. *ancestor*	**mûpu**	(K. *mûppu*=old).
16. *clan*	(No Tuḍa word)	
17. *man, person, husband*	**âl**	
18. *a young man*	**varsh**	(S. *bâla*).
19. *son, boy*	**mokh**	(K. *maga*); **popen.** (?) **tùj mokh**=daughter (§ 23).
20. *woman, girl, daughter, wife*	**kukh**	(? Comp. S. *guhya.* Tam. *kokku, kongu* Perhaps a depreciatory word connected with the root *kug*).
21. *father*	**appn, êyan, en**	(Kan.)
22. *mother*	**avv**	(Kan. *avva*).
23. *wife*	**kâṭvoti**	(Kan. *kattubaḍi* = one bound).
24. *bachelor*	**mokh-varsh**	
25. *child*	**kin mokh** (m.), **tùj-mokh** (f.) (§ 23)	
26. *child* (infant)	**popen** (m.) (?)	
	kin-minthki (f.)	(*Kin.* § 23, *minthki* is of uncertain origin; ? *manushi*: probably a pet word).
27. *twins*	**mor-mokh**	(perhaps *mor* = *marr* = other).
28. *orphan*	**tobbâri**	(K. *tabbili*).
29. *widower*	**baruḍa**	(A. K. *baraḍa*=empty).
30. *widow*	**mudegitti, barudi**	(K *muṇḍe*).
31. *great-grandfather*	**pêvian**	**pî** or **pêvi** +21, 22 — *pî, pêvi,* forms of *piri,* 'great.'
32. *great-grandmother*	**pêviavv**	
33. *grandfather*	**pîyan**	
34. *grandmother*	**pîyavv**	
35. *brother* (younger)	**ennorvet**	(**en**=my, **or**=one, **vet**= *petta,* which in A. K.= brought forth).
36. *brother* (elder)	**ennaṇ**	(*en*+*an.* Kan.).
37. *brother* or *sister* (younger)	**enta**	(Lit.=that one).

38.	*sister* (elder)	**en akka**	(Kan.).
39.	*mother-in-law, father's sister*	**mâmi**	(Kan.).
40.	*father-in-law, mother's brother*	**mâman**	(Kan.).
41.	*son's wife*	**mortwirth**	(? Tam. *maru-magaḷ*).
42.	*daughter's husband*	**enman mokh**	
43.	*father's brother* (elder)	**ennan perud**	
44.	*father's brother* (younger)	**ennan kirud**	
45.	*mother's sister* (elder)	**perud avv**	
46.	*mother's sister* (younger)	**kirud avv**	
47.	*husband's brother* (elder)	**yen âl ennan**	
48.	*husband's brother* (younger)	**yen âl norvet**	
49.	*wife's sister* (elder)	**yen kâtvoti akkan**	
50.	*wife's sister* (younger)	**yen kâtvoti norvet kukh**	
51.	*wife's brother*	**pâyâl**	

52.	*spear*	**îṭ**	(Kan.).
53.	*bow*	**virzh**	(§ 7).
54.	*arrow*	**âbu**	(Kan., Tam., Tel., Mal. *ambu*. Here the Tuḍa has dropped *m*, and lengthened the vowel, as compensation.)
55.	*knife*	**tûri**	(K. *dûru*, go through).
56.	*club*	**kunḍu**	(K. *gunḍu*).
57.	*net*	**balle**	(K. *bâle*).
58.	*axe*	**mosht**	(? A. Tam. *moṛi*).
59.	*hatchet*	**kûrvâl**	(K. *kûr*=sharp; *bâl-u*= knife. This is the exact Tamil; a Poligar word?).

N. B.—No Tuḍa word for *cow*, *plough*, *sword*, or *shield*.

CHAP. XXIX.

No.	English	Tuda	Notes
60.	*buffalo* (male)	**êsht**	(*ĕrru*=ascend, is the Drâv. for the male of any animal).
61.	*buffalo* (female)	**er**	(Kan. *emme*. Tam. *erumai*. Mal. *erima*. Tel. *enumu*).
62.	*calf* (male)	**koan**	(Kan. *kand-u*=a calf).
63.	*calf* (female)	**karr**	(K. *karu*=a calf.)
64.	*deer*	**mâf**	(Dr. *mân*).
65.	*dog*	**nai**	(Kan.)
66.	*dog* (wild)	**chen-nai**	(Red-dog, § 23).
67.	*cat*	**kotti**	(Kan. *kotti*).
68.	*tiger*	**pürsh**	(§ 7).
69.	*bear*	**karsh**	(§ 8).
70.	*snake*	**pàb**	(Kan. *pâv-u*. Tam. *pâmb-u*. Tel. *pàm-u*).
71.	*mouse*	**irzh**	(Kan. *ili*=a rat).
72.	*bird*	**bilti**	(Kan. *beḷ* seems to be the root of it).
73.	*crow*	**kàk**	(Kan.).
74.	*sparrow*	**gubbi bilti**	(See 72. Kan. *gubbi*=sparrow).
75.	*fish*	**mîn**	(Kan.).
76.	*insect*	**pûf**	(§ 9).
77.	*butterfly*	**kappan**	(?).
78.	*louse*	**pên**	(Kan.).
79.	*bird's nest*	**bilt-gûdu**	(Kan.).
80.	*bird's egg*	**much**	(Tam. *muṭṭai*. Kan. *guḍḍu*).
81.	*village*	**mand, madd**	(K. *mande*=herd).
82.	*house, room*	**ârsh**	(*âri* = ring, circular enclosure, or *arrai*=room, in Drâv.).
83.	*cattle-pen*	**tuel**	(Dr. *toṛu* = fold. A. K. *turu*=cow).
84.	*dairy*	**pâlthchi**	(*pâl*+?).
85.	*village-wall*	**tuar**	(Tam. *ṭuvar*; *ṭ* and *t* are interchangeable).
86.	*fire-place*	**vorsh, vorsh-kâll**	(K. *ole*. § 6).
87.	*milk-pail*	**honnu**	(? Tam. *pânê*).
88.	*cattle-bell*	**konku** or **kong, gette**	
89.	*milk*	**pâl**	(A. K. *pâl*).

90. *ghee* (clarified butter)	**nei**	(A. K. *neyi*).
91. Affixes to names of villages	**gadu, gudu, iri, ari**	Drâ. *kuḍi*=tenancy, habitation, **iri, ari,** from root *er*.

---

92. *head*	**madd**	(K. *maṇḍe*).
93. *skull*	**madd-uvar**	
94. *face*	**konmun**	
95. *eye*	**kannu**	(K.).
96. *nose*	**mituf**	(*miṭṭe*, a projection+?).
97. *mouth*	**bâi**	(K.).
98. *ear*	**kevi**	(K. *kivi*).
99. *tooth*	**parsh**	(K. *pal-lu*, § 6).
100. *hand*	**kei**	(K.).
101. *foot*	**kâl**	(K.).
102. *finger*	**belḥ**	(K. *beraḷ-u*)
103. *toe*	**kâl belḥ**	(=foot-finger).
104. *navel*	**pokku**	(A. Kan. *pokkuḷ-u*).
105. *blood*	**bâkh**	(?) The word means *red*, comp. *râg*.
106. *membrum virile*	**bodd**	(Kan.).
107. *pudendum muliebre*	**âkukh, kuk**	(= a receptacle; comp. 20).

---

108. *God, Lord, High Lord*	**dêr, swâmi, ûsuru swâmi**	(K. *dêvar-u swâmi* (S.))
109. *demon*	**bhût**	S.
110. *ghost*	**bhût**	S.
111. *idol*	(No Tuḍa word)	
112. *heaven*	**amnôr**	(? *a*=that; § 21; *nâd*=region).
113. *right*	**sari**	(Kan.)
114. *sin*	**pâpam**	(S.).
115. *life*	**dsivl**	(? S. and Dr. *jîva*: also the organs of generation in a polite way).
116. *breath*	**dîv**	
117. *relic*	**kurpu, mani**	(A.K. *kurupu*=sign, *maṇi*=bell. Every **maṇi** is a **kurpu**, but every **kurpu** is not a **maṇi**).

CHAP. XXIX.

118. *Toda sanctum*	**tiriêri**	(K. *tiru* = sacred, *are* = place. Comp. Sâxon *dry*=a magician, druid).
119. *temple* (conical)	**boath, boa**	(? The words *booth* and *bothy* present a curious resemblance).
120. *sacred shrub*	**tûre, tûde, zhûre**	(S. *tulasi*, the 'Ocymum sanctum').
121. *bell-god*	**maṇi-dêr, konku-dêr, get-dêr**	(Comp. 88, 108, 117).
122. *head priest*	**pâlâl**	(=milkman).
123. *sacrificing priest*	**vorshâl**	(=man of the fireplace).
124. *sacred dairyman*	**pâlkârpâl**	
125. *sacred herdsman*	**kâvilâl**	
126. *religious custom*	**shâstr**	(S.).

---

127. *a kairn*	**vinn**	(A. K. *vind-u*=a heap).
128. *a kromleck*	(No Tuḍa name)	Termed 'stonedairies' or 'little houses.'
129. *funeral*	**kêḍu**	(Kan.=destruction).
130. *place of final obsequies*	**âthârm, âthâre, âthârb**	(? S. *âdhâram*).
131. *ashes* (human)	**nîrrzh**	(Drâ. *nîrru*).
132. *ashes*	**bûdi**	(Kan. *bûdi*, from S. *vib-'hûti*).

---

133. *day of 24 hours*	**nâḷ**	(Drâ.).
134. *to-day*	**êddu**	(Kan. *ind-u*).
135. *yesterday*	**ennêr**	(Kan. *ninne.* Tam. *nêttu*).
136. *to-morrow*	**makâl**	(? + S. *kâla*=time).
137. *a week*	**eṭṭnâḷ**	(=eight days).
138. *a month*	**mupath nâḷ**	(=thirty days).
139. *a month*	**deltu**	(? A. K. *tingaḷu*=moon).
140. *a year*	**vâr**	(K. corruption of *varusha*).
141. *dawn*	**belkâshk**	(=when the morning star is seen. Comp. 146, 153).
142. *dawn*	**êrigitâshk**	(=rising time. Comp. 146. K. *êru*=rise).
143. *sunrise*	**bîrshabât, bîrshkâshk**	(Comp. 148).
144. *noon; daytime*	**pachal**	(S. Kan. *pagal-u*).

CHAP. XXIX.

145. *sunset*	**êkarvâshk**	(Comp. 146. ? *êgu*=go).
146. *night, bedtime*	**îr, îrzh, îrzhtâshk**	(Drâv. *irulu* = darkness. *âshk* in all these words is of uncertain origin. It is probably a corruption of *kâlam* = time, and seems to be *kâshk*).
147. *midnight*	**nadujâma**	(Kan.=middle watch).
148. *sun*	**bîrsh**	(K. *bisul-u*).
149. *moon*	**tiggalu**	(Comp. 139).
150. *new moon*	**muṭṭu**	(? *muttu*=pearl; *muṭṭu*=touch).
151. *star*	**mîn**	Dr.=the twinkler).
152. *sky*	**bân**	(Kan.).
153. *light*	**beḷak, beḷk**	(Kan. *beḷa-k-u*).
154. *darkness*	**irzh**	(Comp. 146).
155. *lightning*	**mijju**	(Kan. *minug-u*).
156. *rainbow*	**kvarvarvirsh**	(Comp. 53, 159).
157. *rain*	**mlâ**	(K. *maḷe*).
158. *wind*	**kâtu**	(Tam. *kâttu*. K. *gâḷi*).
159. *storm with rain*	**kvar**	(K. *kâru*=the wet season).
160. *shadow*	**naḷ, nerzh**	(K. *neḷal-u, neralu*).
161. *smoke*	**pokh**	(A. K. *poge*).
162. *thunder*	**yerthti**	(=it thunders).
163. *fire*	**nebbu, diṭṭh**	
164. *mantle*	**putkuḷi**	(A. K. *podda-kambaḷi*=a blanket in wear).
165. *cloth to pass under the legs.* The lungoti	**kûvn**	(S. *kaupîna*).
166. *bracelet*	**pall, ebball**	(K. *baḷe*).
167. *armlet*	**tûḷwaji**	(K. *toḷwanki*).
168. *necklace*	**kavich**	(Drâv. use of S. *kavacha*).
169. *neck-ring*	**belthta**	(Comp. 170).
170. *finger-ring*	**belth**	(Comp. 102, prob. from *baḷe*=a fillet. The Kan. roots *baḷ, beḷ*).
171. *ear-ring* (silver)	**kev-belth**	(=ear-ring).
172. *ear-ring* (gold)	**dsin, dseṭṭi**	K. *chinna*=gold).
173. *tattoo marks*	**gurtu**	(K. *kuruh-u*; *gurtu*)

CHAP. XXIX.

174. *hill*	**diṭu**	(K. *tiṭṭa*)
175. *valley*	**kli**	(K. *kîḷ*).
176. *river*	**par**	(A. K. *pari-yu*, flow).
177. *forest*	**koar, mên**	(K. *kâḍ-u* ; *mara*).
178. *tree, wood*	**mên**	(K. *mara*).
179. *bush*	**tapi, tûre**	(Comp. 120).
180. *grass*	**pullu**	(A. Kan.)
181. *flower*	**pu**	(A. Kan.)
182. *fruit*	**pôm**	(A.K. *paṇṇ-u*. Tam. *paṛam*. S. P'HAḶAM).
183. *juice*	**kar, nîr**	(K. S. *sâra*. 184).
184. *water*	**nîr**	(K. *nîru*).
185. *mud*	**purzh**	(K. *burude*, § 6).
186. *soil*	**mannu**	

---

187. *gold*	**dsin**	(K. *chinna*).
188. *silver*	**beḷthti**	(K. *beḷḷi*).
189. *iron*	**kabban**	(Kan.).
190. *brass*	**tembu**	(K. *chembu*).
191. *lead*	**disal**	(S. Drâv. *sîsa*).
192. *stone*	**karah**	(K. *kall-u*).

---

193. *north* 194. *south*	The Tuḍas have no word for 'north' and 'south,' but say only 'here' and 'there'; **ite** and **ate**.	
195. *east*	**kîrah, mûralu**	(Kan. *mûda*, *kîḷ*).
196. *west*	**blui**	=place of the sun's setting.
	mok	=above. (Tending to show that the Tuḍas originally lived on the eastern or lower side of the ghâts)
197. *wet season*	**kuar**	(K. *kâr*).
198. *dry season*	**baram**	(Kan. *bara*, dry).

Here **vom**=*vâram*. (S.)

199. *Sunday*	**âsvom**	*âs* (?)
200. *Monday*	**tuvom**	*tu* (?)
201. *Tuesday*	**âm**	(?)
202. *Wednesday*	**budavom**	*buda*=Mercury (S.)

203. *Thursday* **tâm** (?) CHAP. XXIX.
204. *Friday* **beḻḻivom** *beḻḻe*=silver, a name of Venus.
205. *Saturday* **thanivom** *thani*=*sani.* (S.)

A few of the words in this list defy all attempts to trace their origin. And this is not surprising. If in English such words as *boy*, *girl*, *dog*, and *pig*, though modern, cannot be traced, a tribe like the Tuḍas may well have invented a few terms.

§ 42. TUḌA NUMERALS.

I.	**vodd**	(K. *ond-u*)
II.	**edd**	(K. *eraḍu*)
III.	**mûdu**	(K. *mûr u*)
IV.	**nânku**	(K. *nâlk-u.* T. *nâng-u*)
V.	**ütsh**	(K. *eid-u*)
VI.	**âr**	(K. *âru*)
VII.	**êlzh**	(K. *êḻ-u.* T. *êṛ-u*)
VIII.	**eṭṭ**	(K. *enṭ-u.* T. *eṭṭ-u*)
IX.	**onpath**	(K. *on-batt-u*)
X.	**pattu**	(A. K. *pattu*)
XII.	**ponedd**	(A. K. *paneraḍ-u*)
XVI.	**pârzh**	(A. K. *padinâr-u*)
XX.	**êvoth**	(K. *ippattu*)
XXX.	**mûpath**	(K. *mûvattu*)
XL.	**nâlpath**	(K. *nâlvattu*)
L.	**epath**	(K. *eivattu*)
C.	**nûr**	(K. *nûru*).

§ 43. A few subjects for discussion may be indicated here.

(1) In examining these lists I think it will become evident that the 'lingual' or 'cerebral' letters in the Drâviḍian languages are all corruptions of one letter, a kind of l. This seems to be the one Vêdic cerebral.

Kan. *maḻal-u* is Tam. *maṇal*, so
Kan. *maḻai* is Tam. *maṛai*
Kan. *nâḍ* is Tuḍa *naṛ*.

Comp. §§ 6–8.

CHAP. XXIX.

The Drâvidian languages had originally one cerebral, as had the Sanskrit and the Welsh.

(2) The Tuda *temporal particles* (§ 28) are

k for the *present* (**ch, sh, h**)
th (sharp) for the *past* (**d**)
b for the *future* (**p, v**) (only obscurely indicated)

It is perhaps in vain to form conjectures as to the origin of these, but **k** seems allied to **ge** or **ke**=do;

th may be connected with the root **tâ, dâ, d'hâ**=*give, place, establish.*
b is possibly allied to S. *b'hu* and its cognates.

(3) The Tuḍa nominal inflectional particles, or case endings, are (§§ 15–17) at the most four:

g (k); edd (end); ad; orzh.

Of these **g** I connect with **ge**=do;

edd (end=erd) is past of **er**=be;
ad (ath) is adj. pronoun;
orzh (or) is the root of a verb, signifying *absolute existence.*

§ 44. On the whole I venture to think that

(1) The Tuḍa is a language which was once highly inflectional; but, having lost most of its inflections, the people, who have evidently degenerated in every way as the result of isolation, have not replaced them by significant particles or auxiliaries to the same extent as the other South-Indian tribes; and the language has thus dwindled down to a mere skeleton. It now barely suffices for the purposes of a very barbarous people.

(2) The language seems to have been originally Old Kanarese, and not a distinct dialect The Tudas were probably immigrants from the Kanarese country; and have dwelt on the Nîlagiris for about 800 years. Their language was Old Kanarese. A few Tamil forms were introduced by

the Poligars. Intercourse with the Baḍagars has probably modernized a few of the forms and introduced some words. Of Telugu influences I see no trace. It is true that the Tuḍa for *tree* is **mân**, and in Telugu *mânu*, while in Tam. and Kan. it is *mara*; but the soft *r* is always avoided by the Tuḍas, who turn *vâram* into *vôm*.

Nor can I trace any resemblance in Tuḍa to Malayalim, in any of the points where that dialect differs from its sisters.

NOTE. Some words have been added to the above list, since the 'outlines' left Dr. Pope's hands. If, in consequence, a few errors have crept into the Chapter, I alone must be held to be responsible for them.—W. E. M.

ADDENDA.

(Translation of Deuteronomy, chap. xxv. 5.)

vodd ennan athum enorvet-mokh vodd-
An elder-brother (and) *his other-born* (younger brother) *in one*

ârzulch uddâdi, vodd, âl mokḥ illâde,
Toda house if they are, one Toda-man a son is not, (childless)

kêdag-pôkadi kêdag-pôkan kâtvodi-kukh en-odd-
if he goes to death (dies) *the dead-one's bound-woman* (wife) *to another*

âlg kattàti, â kukh-âl, enorvet-mokh
man must not join, that woman's man's (husband) *younger-brother*

illaveniâdi, pâyâl â kukh kekhuri vorgma,
or if not, the brother-in-law (near relation) *that woman near shall sleep,*

athum kudma, kâtvodi-âlg enorvet âdi
her shall join, as a wife's man's younger-brother shall he do.